Copyright © by Lon S. Safko

All rights reserved. No part of this book may be used or reproduced by any means, graphic, electronic, or mechanical, including photocopying, recording, taping or by any information storage retrieval system without the written permission of the publisher except in the case of brief quotations embodied in critical articles and reviews.

Printed in the United States of America

This book was created using 100% recycled electrons

No animals were harmed in the making of this book

This book is dolphin safe

I0432188

R.O.I. - R.I.P.
Is Marketing ROI Dead Forever?
Fracture Media

MEDIA

Like any good marketing message, in this six part series, I am going to announce your problem so I can surprise you and get your attention. I will then, describe the problem so you can identify with the problem. Next I will announce the solution so you will want to know more. Then, I am going to describe the solution so you know there's hope. And lastly, I am going to show you where you can find the solution you need. Does this sound like an ED commercial for Viagra?

Are you wondering where your marketing ROI is? Trying to understand why all of the money you invested into traditional marketing isn't showing you a return on investment? Why all of the time and effort you put into social media marketing doesn't seem to be paying off? It's because social media and digital marketing has fractured all media forever.

If you have been doing marketing for as along as I have, then you probably remember when there were only 3 major television networks, one local newspaper, and no more than 5 local radio stations. If you wanted to reach your demographic, you could choose a station or a section of the paper and place your ads. Even if you were a national corporation, the choices were few and you could actually reach most of your audience with a few repetitive ads.

Digital cable television has more than 250 different stations you can advertise on. But, are your customers and prospects "Pawn Stars" fanatics or are they more the "Ice Road Trucker" kind of a crowd. Radio stations have moved from the local home grown stations to the ClearChannel, mega-affiliated syndicated / serious Sirius type stations. So, are your customers more the Howard Stern or the Rush Limbaugh type. And, with literally 1,000's of BlogTalkRadio radio shows, where do, you advertise?

Print has taken it hard over the past half decade as well. In July of 2012, Amazon announced that ebooks had outsold hardcover books and later that same year they announce that ebooks had outsold all printed books together. Even the local newspaper is a thing of the past. The few surviving newspapers are either closed or have become the Rupert Murdock mainstream conglomerate with a continually declining viewership. The reading audience has moved to either ebooks or to one or more of the 181,000,000 blogs instantly available on line. The need for "Fusion Marketing" was needed more than ever.

Then came social media.

View this entertaining video I created that explains why R.O.I. is R.I.P. It's called "Fractured Media":

https://www.youtube.com/watch?v=DqMjHaX59dQ

Then Came Social Media

Like a bullet train from nowhere social media pulled into our stations. We didn't see it coming. We didn't know what to do with it. But, it was here. So many of us jumped on Myspace, then Facebook, signed up for Twitter, got our profiles on LinkedIn, shared some photos on Flickr, and uploaded some videos to YouTube.

Then as marketers, we realized, that with membership numbers as large as we saw, our customers and prospects must be here. We realized as marketers and communicators, we could use this new digital, social media to market our products and services. Just as we have done for the past 6,000 years; every time we invent a new way to communicate, we marketers quickly begin using it to market. It's what we do.

In 1450, Johannes Gutenberg invented his printing press, which democratized the Holy Bible. This took this individually created, hand written, hand illustrated, very expensive form of communication, and brought it to the masses. BlogTalkRadio did the same for people who wanted their own radio show. Blogs did this for those who wanted to be published. YouTube did this for the hidden director in all of us.

Digital media democratized what was previously very expensive forms of communication only available to an elite few and brought it to the masses. Now millions of us could blog about our thoughts and ideas. Millions of us could tweet about what we were having for breakfast. Millions of us could share movies our pets doing tricks. We now has literally hundreds of platforms where we could express ourselves. With this came an even bigger problem, further fracturing.

We had to ask ourselves, were our customers voracious for video but not fascinated by photos? Bonkers for blogs but not titillated by tweets? Fanatical about Facebook but not emotional about e-mail?

With more than 1 billion users of Facebook, there is a good chance that a segment of your customer demographics are there, but what percentage? With more that 200 million users of LinkedIn and and another 200 million+ Twitter users, more than likely, your demographic is represented there as well. Even Mysapce has more than 200 million active users.

So the big question now is, where do you focus your efforts on to reach the greatest number of potential customers with the least amount of effort and expense and the short answer is "everywhere". Because "everywhere" is where your prospects are. Everyone's demographics are everywhere, They are completely fractured.

Email Is Dead, Long Live Email

One of my consulting clients like many other websites was hit by Google's algorithm change Penguin and Panda. If you're not aware of this, Google rolled out major updates on how they rank websites (their algorithm), in November of 2012, just before the holiday shopping season began.

A majority of my client's traffic and revenue was from Google's organic search traffic. In a blink of an eye, their organic search traffic came to a halt. What made it worse was this happened right before the Holiday shopping rush. I believe the word "panic" was an understatement.

If you've done or are at all familiar with SEO, you know that there is no immediate fix to this problem. To salvage the Holiday buying season from the loss of organic search revenue, I had to look at other advertising channels and quickly.

The advertising channel I decided to focus on was email. After all, they already had a solid database of customer and prospects and it's FREE (or nearly). Email marketing has always been part of their marketing mix but it had never really been optimized. I created their entire email campaign strategy.

I looked at segmentation, sales copy, product offerings, open rates, trends, frequency, content day-parting, and more.

The bottom-line… email marketing worked! I was able to instantly fill a great portion of the gap from the loss of organic search revenue using email marketing. If you were able to see the stats compared to the previous year, I believe you would be blown away and take email marketing more seriously.

If you purchased anything as a result of an email you received during the holidays, that proves that email marketing does work! And, Segmenting your customers who have recently purchased, works even better.

The main concern people have about their own email marketing was "TIME". I hear it all of the time, "I just don't have time to develop an email marketing campaign". We all have a problem with too little time. The reality is that you can automate a lot or most of your email process.

Automate you ask? You mean I don't have to respond to every single email? The answer is YES!

With a properly implemented email system, here's what you can actually do with email automation:

- Send your customer a welcome email when they sign up for your list.
- Send your customers a successive (Drip-Feed) weekly email for the next 5 weeks when they join your list.
- Send them product specific sequenced emails if they click on certain links within your email.
- Send a follow-up survey to customers who have made a purchase in the last X days.
- Send your customers coupons after X days of purchasing your product.
- Segment your customers based on their buying habits or what type of information they are looking for.
- Send leads to your sales staff if the customer clicks on certain links.
- Build your list and potential customer database with opt-in forms.

And, this is just only the beginning! Set it and forget it with email marketing automation. Create an automated system that will properly help you guide your your prospects through your sales funnel.

Now, the only thing it can't do is write the email for you but there's an inexpensive way to do that also. Alright, so no more excuses that you don't have enough time! Automate your email campaign!

Free Automation Example

Here's an example of how I use the standard Microsoft email program, Outlook to automate my webinar / white paper delivery system.

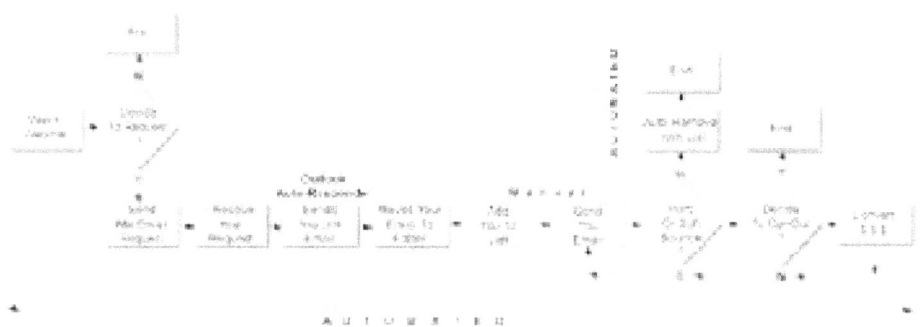

Email Automation Example

I perform webinars on a regular basis. I perform my most requested keynotes and concept from my two bestselling books "The Social Media Bible" and "The Fusion Marketing Bible". I do these webinars so I can continue to build my list. I have to keep adding people to my list, keep it fresh with new eyes, and replace opt-outs that happen with any email list.

Here's what I do using only one simple "Rule" in Outlook:

1. I offer a white paper at the end of my webinar or offer it from my web site.

2. When the viewer decides to get the white paper, they simply send me a request to predetermined email address, such as "requests@TheFusionAcademy.com".

3. When that email is received in in my inbox in Outlook, it is automatically, placed in it's own folder called "White Paper Requests",

4. A special sounds plays to tell me someone has requested the white paper and I have a new opted -in email address.

5. And, Outlook, send each person an email from me with a link to where they can download that paper.

All this without human intervention and absolutely free!

If you used an Email Service Provider such as AWeber, ConstantContact, MailChimp, or Infusionsoft the amount of automation, follow-up, and drip advertising you could do is unimaginable. That level of email automation does come with a price. As little as $14.99 per month to well over a $1,000.

List Building

One of the most important things that marketers tend to forget is that their prospects buy on their time and not your advertisement time. Unless you're buying targeted traffic that is looking to purchase your product at that very moment, getting just "traffic" will not convert very well for you.

I'm not interested in just getting traffic. I'm interested in building my email list, a very big list, and create long term relationships. Many people in my list have been with me for nearly 10 years!

When I can capture a lead, I can "drip-feed" that prospect, continuous information until they are ready to buy without spending a cent more in advertising or upsetting that lead. The prospects that are visiting your site most likely will never come back. Why not maximize that opportunity by capturing that lead.

Here are a few ideas on how you can capture leads:

- Offer coupons and specials

- Have a "light-box" opt-in form that pops up when someone first visits your site with a compelling incentive to register

- Offer access to exclusive content

- Offer more information on certain products

- Offer downloadable case studies or white papers

- Offer an email newsletter with updated industry or subject matter news

- Think of ways to offer your prospect overwhelming value in exchange for their email address. "What in it for them!" or "I didn't Know That!" content.

A good list converts well. A good, large list can create a large reliable revenue stream.

As Mark Twain might have said "The reports of email's death are greatly exaggerated."

Social Media Is Dead

Jeff Elder wrote an article for the Wall Street Journal "Social Media Fail to Live Up to Early Marketing Hype", which was based on a survey done by Gallup the long standing polling company, saying that Social Media hasn't performed as anticipated.

WSJ Article: http://on.wsj.com/1rHYi30

Gallup Poll: http://on.wsj.com/1izsMUu

The article and survey lead with "62% of people participating in social networks say that those networks have no influence on their buying decisions at all."

I read the WSJ article and the Gallup poll, and at first I was astonished as most of the WSJ's readers probably were. Especially all of the social media managers and V.P.'s of Social Media in Fortune 500 companies throughout the U.S. I seriously considered that if these two bastions of business information and integrity said this, it might actually be true, but I instinctually knew better.

Then, I received this email from a reader of my book "The Social Media Bible" who asked this:

"I am a SCORE counselor from Phoenix who specializes in Government contracts. ...I do have a question: a Gallup poll whose results were published recently, seems to conclude that on-line advertising is useless and a waste. Gallup concluded that only a tiny percentage of people even notice them. The study targeted Social media.

Their conclusion: Do not waste time on Facebook, LinkedIn, Twitter or similar services.

http://www.score.org/

I am interested to read your reaction to that extensive survey from such a prestigious organization.
Regards,
Jean Jolkovski in Ahwatukee"

Jean's email question forced me to take a more serious look at these serious accusations before I responded.

My response:

"Hello Jean,
Social media marketing is the same as any marketing. It takes time, resources, and a sound strategy. You have to ask, where's the ROI in print ads or where's the ROI in direct mail. It's in there, that's why we still do it. With social media, we also do it because there is an ROI when it's done correctly. Social media marketing is still marketing and can be effective if done with a strong strategic plan.
Lon"

REASONS FOR SOCIAL MEDIA USE

To connect with friends and family — 94%

To follow trends/To find product reviews and information — 29%

To comment on what's hot or new/To write reviews of products — 20%

Jean replied:

"Yes, of course, any attempt at marketing requires both excellent planning and effective execution if it is to achieve success. Social media marketing does not get a pass from that principle. But, just as it is true when you try to train a mule, it only works if you can get the prospect's attention. An unseen pitch simply does not exist!

As I read the survey, the objective was not an attempt to measure effectiveness. The conclusion was that the message was not even noticed by the audience. It had become simply a part of the noise. That, as I, as a non-expert, see it as the real threshold to be crossed if any Social media campaign is to become effective."

Jean Jolkovski in Ahwatukee"

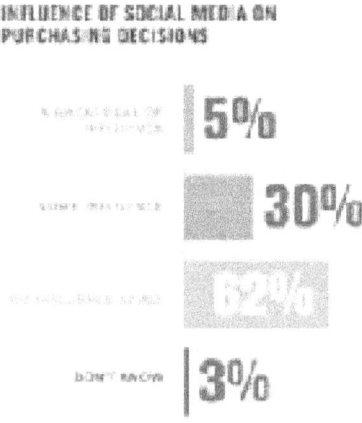

Where The WSJ And Gallup Went Wrong

Here's my reply back:

"I would like to see a Gallup survey measuring the influence television commercials and print ads have on customers. I bet those numbers are even worse. True, with all of the noise out there, it is becoming more difficult to be heard. That's why social media is a good choice.

The poll said that social media has "A great deal of influence on 5% of the people polled". Direct mail has only 1/2 of 1% response rate. That makes social media marketing 10x more effective than direct mail and significantly less expensive to implement.

The poll also says that social media had "Some influence on 30% of the buying decisions of the people polled". I don't think one print ad could possibly influence 35% of its readers. The reason 62% of social media participants polled said that it had no influence was, because the reader (watcher) wasn't ready to purchase that particular product or service. Lon"

This leads back to a concept that is seldom used by marketing people, but is understood by nearly all sales people; The Sales Funnel.

The Famous Sales Funnel

	Frame Of Mind	Goal	Conversion	Example
Awareness		Build Brand Awareness	Very Low	Insurance
Search		Frame Buying Decisions	Low	Car Insurance
Research		Directly Compete	Moderate	Car Insurance Quote
Purchase		Convert To Sales	High	New York Car Insurance Quote

(Sales Cycle)

Just because you saw a truck ad or fast food ad on TV last night, doesn't mean that you ran out and bought a big truck and a Big Mac® this morning before you went to work. The ad had no influence on you whatsoever, because your weren't ready to buy either product. However, when you ARE ready to buy a truck or a burger, you will think of the person / company that is in the forefront of your mind from Facebook, Twitter, LinkedIn, etc., and you will most likely buy from them first. The time that it takes you to go from first realizing that you need a particular product / service (awareness) until the time you actually purchase that product / service is call the Sales Cycle.

For a truck, the sales cycle could be several years and for a pack of chewing gum at the checkout isle it takes only 30 seconds. The cycle is usually proportional to the cost of the item. The truck has a very long cycle the gum, very short. This is why, if you are a truck retailer, you have to stay in front of your prospects often and for a very long time to catch them at the very moment of awareness and influence them.

The The Wall Street Journal article and the Gallup Survey was wrong and has no value from this perspective.

Ask The Experts

I quickly realized that this is a bigger issue than I alone should answer, I sent this email thread to some of my close friends who happen to be top "experts" in social media from around the world. Here's what some of those experts had to say:

"Great article. Sensible companies like the Ritz Carlton are understanding the proper way to harness Social."
Erik Qualman, Motivational Speaker - Digital Leadership, Author of "Socialnomics" @equalman

~ • ~ • ~ • ~ • ~ • ~ • ~

"In response to the WSJ article- Its not terribly surprising that there's a backlash against social media marketing. As in any unregulated industry, you will have some agencies and individuals who do their business superbly, and many who are riding the tide of the latest and greatest, who unfortunately do the industry an injustice, resulting in unhappy customers and unimpressive ROI and results. I know social media marketing works- but its wholly dependent on the skill of the agency and the efforts of the client."
Viveka von Rosen (One Of The Top 50 most influential bloggers.)

~ • ~ • ~ • ~ • ~ • ~ • ~

"Social media can be a waste of time — if you don't know how to use it. The days of broadcasting a bunch of Tweets or Facebook posts are over. Today, social media is much more nuanced and complex and includes everything from native advertising to social listening. In a nutshell, social media is way, way past the "give it to the intern" stage and well into the "give it to a seasoned professional" stage."

Jamie Turner, CEO, Author of "Go Mobile", 60 Second Communications and 60 Second Marketer

~ • ~ • ~ • ~ • ~ • ~ • ~

"That's interesting, but so predictable. Its subheadline says "A MAJORITY OF CONSUMERS SAY THEY ARE NOT INFLUENCED BY FACEBOOK, TWITTER", but if you ask the question "Are you influenced by others opinion on products and services", the answer would be 100% yes, and these "others" are people they know and trust, it would be 200% ;-)

Social is just the channel to convey these opinions and amplify them. It always all depends on the angle of the question..."

Emeric Ernoult, Founder & CEO, <u>Agorapulse</u>, Facebook Marketing & CRM, Paris (France)

~ • ~ • ~ • ~ • ~ • ~ • ~

"The Gallup Poll referenced by the WSJ article is interesting in that 62% of consumers said social does not influence their purchase decisions at all. Consumers don't spend time attributing an item they purchase back to if and when they engaged or viewed brand content on social so it makes sense that 62% of consumers would state that social does not influence purchasing.

When brands focus on creating engaging campaigns that make fans happy the brand wins every time. Torani is doing a great job of this currently, leveraging the World Cup, through a fun and engaging Facebook campaign that is converting fans into email leads at a 75.47% conversion rate.

According to an internal research report done at Heyo, based off a data set of 202 campaigns launched between June 15th and June 21st, the average fan to email lead conversion rate was 12.2% across a sample size of 202 social campaigns. Going from fun and engaging contest to email lead is the first step in the social ROI funnel."

Nathan Latka, Founder & CEO, Heyo, Social Campaigns

~ • ~ • ~ • ~ • ~ • ~ • ~

"Social drives brand equity and sales, it creates an emotional connection with customers and helps build customer loyalty through evangelists, it leads to greater exposure through search. In short it is critical in driving market positioning from the 4Ps (Product, Place, Price and Promotion) that have been in effect since the 50s to the 4Es (Experience, Everywhere, Exchange and Evangelism) Here's my piece on Forbes on the subject: http://goo.gl/htvnf.

Those who go through the trouble to create a general brand-awareness/ audience connecting campaign through social media, see an increase in market share by then implementing very specific campaigns that are linked to short sale cycles. The "Old Spice" adverts that targeted influencers, reached all the way to Oprah and converted a larger slice of the target audience (women) are a case in point. Others are the Johnson & Johnson baby oil campaign in China, Pfizer's dominance of the pharma league table for three years running now, Without a strong social component that is also amplified in search none of these would even have been possible.

Traditional companies with traditional mindsets use social to broadcast expecting it will give them the linear results of the traditional advertising. Well, that is like using a tennis racquet to paddle in the river, because it's the same shape as a paddle. The results will be radically different."

David Amerland, Author, Speaker, Analyst

~ • ~ • ~ • ~ • ~ • ~ • ~

Another great burst of useful information. To many people and corporations need to re-thinking Social Media strategy or tactics. Sounds like they "had to do the **Newest Thing**", with out asking, how does it fit into our marketing strategy.

Gary Thuerk, Speaker & Consultant, Father of E-spam

~ • ~ • ~ • ~ • ~ • ~ • ~

What the WSJ article and Gallup poll should have said was "35% of all people who participate on social networks are influenced at some level to buying your products!" That's more than 1 out of 3!

But I guess that doesn't sell papers or reports…

For more information about the author, please visit
www.LonSafko.com

www.ingramcontent.com/pod-product-compliance
Lightning Source LLC
Chambersburg PA
CBHW050039230526
45470CB00003B/1359